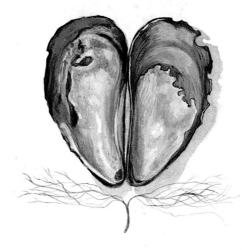

This book belongs to

Martha + John

with love,

Carly Simon

♡ Margot Datz

also by Carly Simon and Margot Datz

Amy the Dancing Bear

The Boy of the Bells

The Fisherman's Song

by

Carly Simon

Illustrated by Margot Datz

DOUBLEDAY

New York   London   Toronto   Sydney   Auckland

PUBLISHED BY DOUBLEDAY
a division of Bantam Doubleday Dell Publishing Group, Inc.
666 Fifth Avenue, New York, New York 10103

DOUBLEDAY and the portrayal of an anchor
with a dolphin are trademarks of Doubleday,
a division of Bantam Doubleday Dell Publishing Group, Inc.

Book design by Marysarah Quinn

Library of Congress Cataloging-in-Publication Data
Simon, Carly.
The fisherman's song/Carly Simon; illustrated by Margot Datz. —
—1st ed.
p.   cm.
Summary: A lyrical tale of an island, and the romance of a man, a
woman, and the sea, based on the song of the same title by Carly Simon.
1. Songs, English – United States – Texts. [1. Songs.] I. Datz,
Margot, ill. II. Title.
PZ8.3.S587Fi 1991
782.42164′0268 – dc 20
91-6653
CIP
AC

ISBN 0-385-41955-4
ISBN 0-385-41957-0 (lib. bdg.)

Text copyright © 1990 by C'Est Music (Carly Simon)
Illustrations copyright © 1991 by Margot Datz
All Rights Reserved
Printed in the United States of America
September 1991

1 3 5 7 9 10 8 6 4 2

First Edition

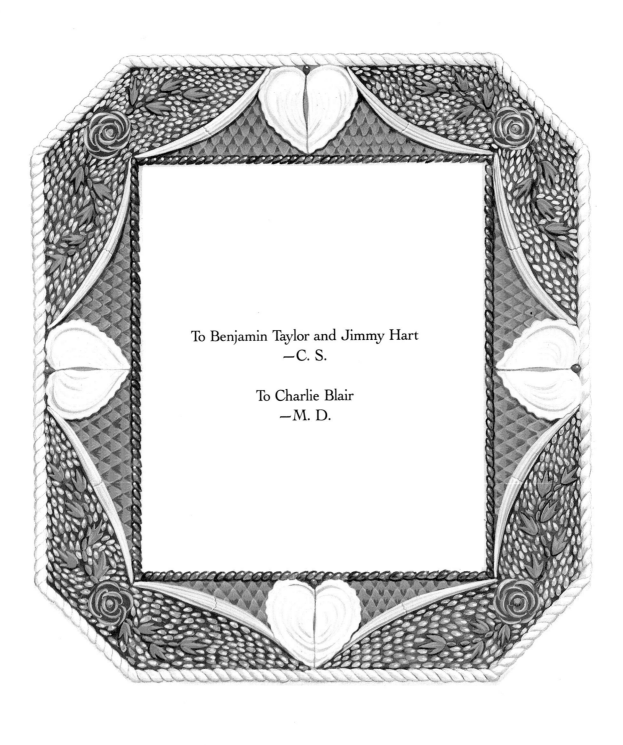

To Benjamin Taylor and Jimmy Hart
—C. S.

To Charlie Blair
—M. D.

In a pine forest, cooler
than the rest of the island,
lives a young fisherman
with eyes like the sea.

He built his own boat
and made his own cabin,
but he's broken the hearts
of the likes of me.

Now you must understand
he made me a promise.
There were secrets we shared,
we planted a tree.

We lived in his cabin,
I fished alongside of him.
I fell under the spell
of his sorcery.

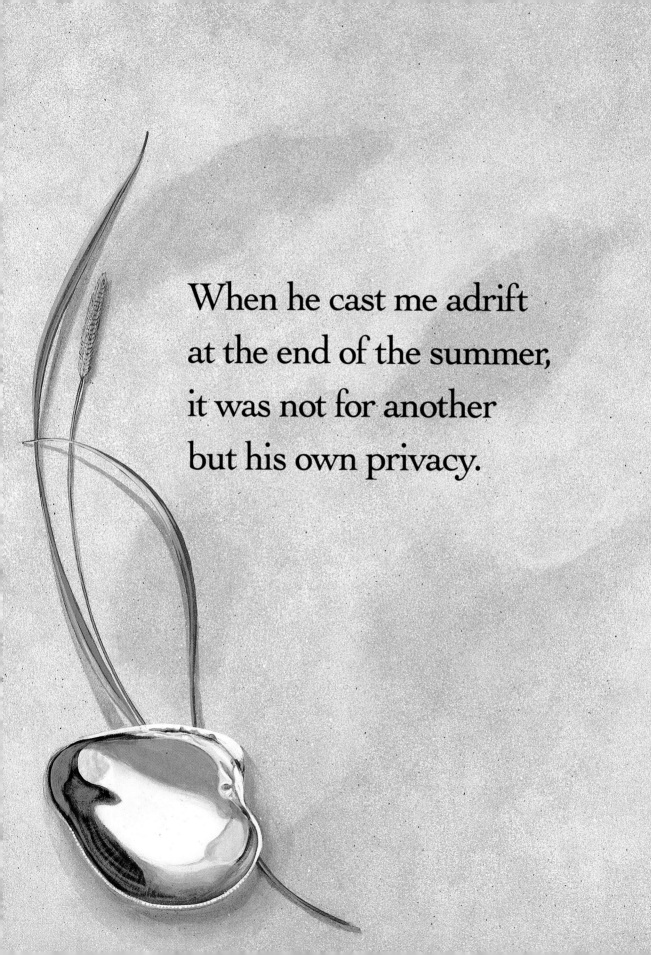

When he cast me adrift
at the end of the summer,
it was not for another
but his own privacy.

I fell apart like a rose,
but the scent of my longing

remains and it weeps
like an old willow tree..

At night when it's still
with the yellow moon rising,
when his candle is snuffed
and he's deep in a dream,

I move like a cat
and crawl into his window
and lie down beside him
in a golden moonbeam.

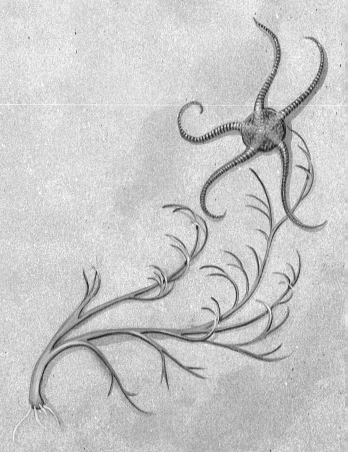

The smell of his skin
is just like the summer,

when our love was as fresh
as the grass in the fields.

And ever so softly
I kiss his eyelids
before slipping away,
my secret concealed.

Though I'm in it alone,
I'm still in it in love
and love can be lonely
like a sweet melody.

But just maybe he feels me
like a whisper inside him,

like an angel beside him,
keeping him company.

Fisherman's Song

Words and Music by
CARLY SIMON

Lyrics:

1. In a pine for-est cool-er than the rest of the is-land lives a young fish-er-man with eyes like the sea. He built his own boat and made his own cab-in, but he's bro-ken the hearts of the likes of me.

2. Now, you... ry. tree.

4. At ooh

Verse 2:
Now you must understand he made me a promise.
There were secrets we shared, we planted a tree.
We lived in his cabin, I fished along side of him.
I fell under the spell of his sorcery.
(To Chorus:)

Verse 3:
When he cast me adrift at the end of the summer,
It was not for another, but his own privacy.
I fell apart like a rose, but the scent of my longing
Remains and it weeps like an old willow tree.

Verse 4:
At night when it's still, with a yellow moon rising,
When his candle is snuffed and he's deep in a dream,
I move like a cat, and crawl into his window
And lie down beside him in a golden moonbeam.
(To Chorus:)

Verse 5;
The smell of his skin is just like the summer,
When our love was as fresh as the grass in the fields.
And ever so softly I kiss his eyelids
Before slipping away, my secret concealed.

Verse 6:
Though I'm in it alone, I'm still in it, in love.
And love can be lonely like a sweet melody.
But just maybe he feels me like a whisper inside him,
Like an angel beside him, keeping him company.
(To Chorus:)